Thames there, was from 1705 to 1869 a home for old and injured seamen: even fewer that, while it no longer occupies the buildings, Greenwich Hospital still exists as a Crown charity that supports seafarers and their families to the extent of some £7 million a year (2009 figures).

This short history of the Hospital was first published in 1994, to mark its 300th anniversary. Since then much has changed at Greenwich, where the Royal Naval College has now also left Wren's buildings after 125 years of occupation (1873–1998). This new edition takes the opportunity to make minor corrections and bring the story up to date in the 21st century.

Foundation, funds and 'fabrick'

'THE DARLING OBJECT'

In November 1694 Samuel Pepys, long retired as Secretary to the Admiralty, wrote to his old friend John Evelyn, formerly of Deptford. His letter touched on the scheme then afoot to build a Royal Naval Hospital at Greenwich, equivalent to that opened in 1692 at Chelsea to house disabled and elderly soldiers. In this Evelyn had been involved, from his 1660s experience as one of the Navy's Commissioners for the sick, wounded and prisoners-of-war. It foreshadowed his even greater connection with Greenwich.

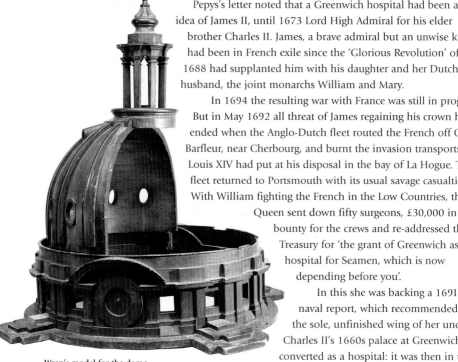

Wren's model for the dome of King William's Court, about 1702.*

Pepys's letter noted that a Greenwich hospital had been an idea of James II, until 1673 Lord High Admiral for his elder brother Charles II. James, a brave admiral but an unwise king, had been in French exile since the 'Glorious Revolution' of 1688 had supplanted him with his daughter and her Dutch husband, the joint monarchs William and Mary.

In 1694 the resulting war with France was still in progress. But in May 1692 all threat of James regaining his crown had ended when the Anglo-Dutch fleet routed the French off Cape Barfleur, near Cherbourg, and burnt the invasion transports Louis XIV had put at his disposal in the bay of La Hogue. The fleet returned to Portsmouth with its usual savage casualties. With William fighting the French in the Low Countries, the Queen sent down fifty surgeons, £30,000 in bounty for the crews and re-addressed the Treasury for 'the grant of Greenwich as a hospital for Seamen, which is now depending before you'.

In this she was backing a 1691 naval report, which recommended that the sole, unfinished wing of her uncle Charles II's 1660s palace at Greenwich be converted as a hospital: it was then in use as a gunpowder store. The Queen now made the idea 'the darling object of her life'. Sir Christopher Wren, the Surveyor-General, was called in, assisted by his clerk, Nicholas Hawksmoor. He offered to design the hospital without charge, as work 'too near akin to him to let it want any degree of furtherance he could give it'.

Wren initially proposed a building round three sides of a courtyard and open to the river on the fourth side, as in his army hospital at Chelsea. One version of this would have blocked the view from Inigo Jones's earlier Queen's House to the river, which it only gained when Charles II demolished the old Tudor palace at Greenwich, and still enjoys. Other opinion suggested that Charles's unfinished building, put up by Jones's pupil John Webb, should also be demolished. Mary, however, ordered that the Queen's House retain its new 'visto' and, 'with as much Indignation as her excellent good Temper would suffer her' (as Hawksmoor put it) also rejected the demolition of her uncle's building. Wren's design had to accommodate both.

The Queen showed economic sense. Wren's agreed plan of four 'courts', with room for 2044 Pensioners, was four times the size of Chelsea Hospital. If Mary had not suddenly died from smallpox in December 1694, the project could still have foundered on its costs and the King's lack of interest. But the tragedy spurred William to appoint first a commission of fourteen, then one of two hundred, to carry her dream forward. The founding charter, backdated in both their names to 25 October, stated the Hospital's purpose as:

John Evelyn, 1620–1706. Writer, diarist, royal adviser on seamen's welfare and first Treasurer of the Hospital, 1695–1703.

> the reliefe and support of Seamen serving on board the Ships and Vessells belonging to the Navy Royall... who by reason of Age, Wounds or other disabilities shall be uncapable of further service...and unable to maintain themselves. And for the sustentation of the Widows and the Maintenance and Education of the Children of Seamen happening to be slain or disabled. Also for the further reliefe and Encouragement of Seamen and Improvement of Navigation.

The 'sustentation of Widows' in the Hospital was never achieved in the buildings' 165 years of use, though some were housed and employed as nurses and domestics, and the educational role was slow to flower. None the less, with the 74-year-old John Evelyn appointed Treasurer, planning began.

On 30 June 1696, Wren, Evelyn and eleven Commissioners

5

Governor Jennings shows a plan of the Hospital to the Prince of Wales: an early sketch for the Upper Hall by Thornhill, bottom right, about 1722.*

dined at Greenwich. 'After dinner at 5 o'clock', wrote Evelyn, 'Mr [John] Flamsteed the King's Astronomical Professor observing the punctual time by instruments' they watched workmen lay the foundation stone of the 'base' building, the new western range which converted Webb's 1660s block into what became King Charles's Court. The bricks used were supplied by a Mr Foe, later to be known as Daniel Defoe, author of *Robinson Crusoe*. This was also the site of the Hospital's last as well as first major construction work. In 1812–15 Wren's base wing was replaced by the then Surveyor, John Yenn's, handsome Regency version.

EVELYN AND THE FABRICK COMMITTEE

Fifty-five years elapsed from the ceremony of June 1696 to the completion in 1751 of the Hospital's last great court, Queen Mary's. However, the building sequence is simple compared to the early organization of the work.

King William's Commission appointed a Grand Committee of sixty. This in turned formed three Committees to work out the Hospital's constitution, raise money and supervise erection of the 'fabrick'. The Constitution and Revenue Committees proved ineffectual and, in practice, the whole burden rested on the Fabrick Committee. This was led by Wren but its key member was the Hospital Treasurer, John Evelyn. When he stood down, aged 83 in 1703, he had been a close royal adviser on building at Greenwich and on sailors' welfare for forty years. In nearly the last ten this scholarly old man kept the project afloat and moving forward. He never took the salary allowed and contributed £2000 to the work, half of it outright just before his death in 1706: it was then found the Hospital still owed him money. The buildings are as much his monument as Queen Mary's.

The first big organizational change also came in August 1703. Mary's sister, Queen Anne, created the Hospital's General Court, chaired (as was the earlier Commission) by her husband Prince George of Denmark, now Lord High Admiral. Under it a new board of Directors was to manage the project. Wren was its first Chairman and the membership was committed and competent. For running the Hospital, the posts of Governor and Lieutenant-Governor were envisaged, with a Council of the other Hospital officers, chaplains and senior medical staff. This structure was to last for 126 years. Among the new Directors was Captain John Clements, a former captain in the royal yachts, who was nominated by Prince George as first Lieutenant-Governor, though he died within months of taking up residence. In January 1705, he moved into the near-complete King Charles Court, with the first 42 Greenwich Pensioners following in June.

THE QUESTION OF MONEY

Building was expensive and funding unreliable. For nearly forty years the project ran up massive deficits and bad example started at the top. In 1695 the leading subscriber, King William, promised £2000 a year 'as a further instance of Our Princely Zeal for advancing the Designe'. His first £2000 only arrived in 1697 and then not in cash but in credits against the Malt Tax, which contractors would not accept at full value. This continued and other subscribers reneged on promises even more. At the end of the first season Evelyn had only received £800 to pay for £5000 of work. The pattern became typical and was mirrored in the Hospital's disjointed progress. By 1703 just under £90,000 had been received, more had been spent and an estimated £128,500 was needed to finish. In 1759 the costs of the finished buildings were reckoned at £400,000, apart from those of fulfilling the Hospital's aims: by 1708 only 300 pensioners had been admitted with 40 staff, all costing £7000 a year and rising as more came. In 1752 Pensioners numbers stood at 1400 and by 1779 there were 2350, excluding out-pensioners and other dependants.

Other sources of money were varied and some very unusual. Since 1590 seamen had paid a welfare deduction of sixpence a month from wages into the Chatham Chest, itself fully amalgamated with the Hospital in 1814. From 1696 a further sixpence was taken for the Hospital. In 1697 the king handed over some £10,500 of fines on French merchants for smuggling and £6472 came from Queen Anne in 1706, being the confiscated property of the executed pirate, Captain William Kidd. The Directors long aspired to take over the Queen's House, its gardens and even the Park for expansion. In 1697–99, the Park

The Chapel fire, 2 January 1779. A print published by Thomas Furbor, then master of the Hospital School.

Pensioners in Fisher's Alley, by Clarkson Stanfield, 1848. When painted, the Hospital had already demolished the area. Stanfield was the first Curator of the Painted Hall, 1844–67.*

Ranger, Lord Romney, hemmed in the Hospital's southward ambitions by building the present Romney Road but in 1700 ceded it his right to establish a market in Greenwich: the Hospital has exercised this since 1737. A lottery was tried in 1699, the Hospital being exempted from a general ban on them. The return was slow but eventually raised nearly £11,500. From 1707 it was further granted all unclaimed Naval Prize Money, which proved valuable during the eighteenth-century wars, and in 1710 Parliament allocated £6000 a year from the revenues of Coal Tax.

Private bequests also figured. The most spectacular was the legacy of Robert Osboldston of Greenwich, who in 1714 left £20,000 of property and the annual dues paid by ships passing his North and South Foreland Lighthouses. From 1728 to 1751 Parliament granted £10,000 a year towards the building and from 1819 the Hospital also benefited from a share of the freight on gold and jewels, then often carried for merchants by Royal Navy ships. This produced some £13,000 a year. From early on the Hospital bought adjacent property in Greenwich to expand its site and in the nineteenth century most of its sources of official funding were translated into interest-bearing Government stocks.

What turned out to be the most important and lasting asset came in 1735. In 1716, James Radcliffe, the handsome young Earl of Derwentwater, was executed as a political example for supporting the Jacobite rising of 1715. His vast estates in Cumberland, Westmorland and Northumberland were confiscated to the Crown, which avoided further unpopularity by eventually giving them to the Hospital. Their mineral wealth, especially in coal and lead (also used for roofing the Hospital) proved increasingly valuable as the industrial revolution advanced. Yielding £7182 in 1734 the 'Northern Estates' were producing £25,000 in 1787 and £39,000 in 1859, even after the sale of large tracts of land.

BUILDING THE HOSPITAL

Dr Johnson thought the four courts of the Hospital 'too much detached to make one great whole' but his view has been a minority one. 'The relation between the blocks of Greenwich Palace, including the placing of the domes, is a great achievement in abstract composition', wrote the architect Professor (Sir) Charles Reilly in 1923:

There is an austerity about Greenwich, with its long, straight, free-standing colonnades, its twin domes, simpler and more graceful in outline than his great one [St Paul's], not to be found in his earlier work. As seen from the river, [it] is one of the most sublime sights English architecture affords... a world of clear expressive shapes, where no careless or muddled efforts exist...

Stuart and Newton's Chapel interior, 1782–88, with Benjamin West's altarpiece of St Paul shipwrecked on Malta.

The final compliment is the more striking given the number of hands involved and the stop-go progress. Construction took place in four main periods with finishing works in between:

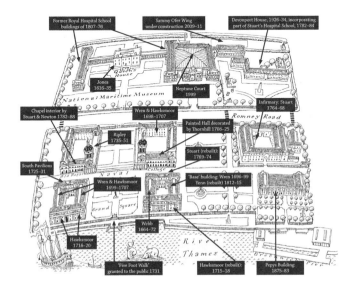

The Hospital site at its full extent by *c.* 1845. The Pepys Building, bottom right, now holds 'Discover Greenwich' (the World Heritage Site visitor centre) the Greenwich Tourist Information Centre and the 'Old Brewery'. Devonport House, now a conference hotel, stands on the old Hospital burial ground of 1749–1857.

1696–1708

In this period the whole foundations were first laid out round the 270ft (83m) 'Grand Square' at the river end, with Mary's sacred 115ft wide (35m) 'visto' continuing south toward the Queen's House. The 'base' (west) wing of the King Charles Court was built to supplement Webb's existing east range of the 1660s; also King William's Court, with the Painted Hall, but excluding the roof of the colonnades and work inside the West Dormitory. The shells of the two ranges of Queen Anne's Court went up in brick, the 'greater' one overlooking Grand Square remaining unfaced. All this was done by Wren, assisted by the Hospital Clerk of Works, Hawksmoor, except the eastern range of Queen Anne which Hawksmoor perhaps designed alone. The western range of King William is now attributed mainly to Hawksmoor rather than (as earlier thought) Sir John Vanbrugh, who became a Hospital Director in 1703 but only succeeded Wren as Surveyor in 1716. Thornhill decorated the Painted Hall ceiling, 1708–12 , and in 1707 Hawksmoor built a temporary chapel between the two Queen Anne ranges.

1712–21

In these years King William's Court was largely completed, Thornhill finishing the Painted Hall decoration, 1718–25. The

Below: The Hospital had some black Pensioners, though only John Deman (d. 1873) is yet known by name. This rare image of one in the 18th-century uniform, is from a drawing by John Thurston, about 1800.
Below right: A 'canary'. A Pensioner wearing the yellow coat as punishment for drunkenness. The standing figure on the right is a Hospital boatswain; from a painting by H. J. Pidding, 1844.

north 'pavilion' of Wren's King Charles base wing was replaced in stone and the linked north pavilions of Queen Anne's Court put up, though not finished internally. All three were organized by Hawksmoor, copying the northern end of Webb's 1660s King Charles wing.

1725–32

Queen Anne's Court was finished internally except the south pavilions which were built as shells; its western range also received its stone facade. Most of this work was done under Colen Campbell, who became Surveyor on Vanbrugh's death in 1726 but himself died in 1729. Then, when money was at last becoming available to finish the Hospital, political jobbery saw Thomas Ripley rather than Hawksmoor

'John Rosedale, Mariner,' 1807. The official guide to the Painted Hall in action; etched by Rowlandson, after John Nixon.

appointed to succeed him. Ripley was an efficient architect rather than a distinguished one and Hawksmoor retired, disappointed, in 1732. In 1731 the public were first granted use of the 'Five-Foot Walk' along the river in front, so-called from its width.

1735–51

In 1735 the Hospital gained the Derwentwater estates. Ripley then completed the south pavilions of Queen Anne and totally built the Queen Mary Court, including the Chapel. The stone eastern range is the dullest design on the site but the whole is very well built, closely copying Wren's King William scheme to north and west, and originally including an elegantly plain chapel with a coffered ceiling. Hawksmoor's temporary chapel was demolished in 1751.

James 'Athenian' Stuart, Surveyor from 1758, rebuilt the south pavilion of Wren's King Charles base range in 1769–74, at the same time as his new Hospital Infirmary (1764–68) on new ground west of the King William Court. This was the first expansion outside the Hospital's original constricted site. It was only in the 1830s that the waterfront tenements between Infirmary and river were cleared and the area taken into the Hospital grounds. Finally, from 1782 to his death in 1788 Stuart directed restoration of the Chapel after it was burnt out, with five adjacent wards, in a catastrophic fire of January 1779. A masterpiece of the Greek-revival style for which he was famed, most of its detailed work was in fact done by his poorly credited Clerk of Works, William Newton. It reopened in 1789, a century after the coronation of the Hospital's royal founders.

'Safely moor'd
in Greenwich Hospital'

THE PENSIONERS

The standard image of Greenwich Pensioners is of peg-legged Nelsonic veterans in blue frock coats and tricorn hats, re-fighting old wars amid ale tankards and the smoke of their long 'chalks' (clay pipes). However, their first uniform – adopted over forty years before the Navy had one – was dark grey with a blue baize lining and brass buttons. In 1712–14 when grey proved difficult to keep clean, uniforms changed to brown and only later to blue. In Sir Thomas Hardy's time as Governor (1834–39) trousers replaced knee-breeches and a round rather than cocked hat was later allowed for normal use.

BED AND BOARD

Pensioner John Adams, aged 78, formerly of Nelson's *Agamemnon*; by Frederick Cruikshank, 1840.

Accommodation in the four courts or 'Quarters' of the Hospital was in wards with naval names. Some of these changed over time and a good many not only survive on door lintels but are still used to identify the rooms concerned. Those of King Charles Court recalled the 17th-century Dutch Wars : 'Royal Charles', 'Monck', and 'Restoration' for example. Of later wards, 'Anson' was from 1836 dominated by the preserved lion figurehead of his ship *Centurion* (subsequently destroyed). 'Franklin' commemorated the lost Arctic explorer, whose 1858 monument, originally in the Painted Hall's entry vestibule, was in 2009 resited in the Chapel's, after being generally invisible in its sacristy since 1938. Each ward was partitioned into 'cabins', for single occupants or small groups. With up to 2710 in-Pensioners, each wore a numbered tally identifying where he belonged in the Hospital. The sick were cared for in infirm wards but in 1764 Stuart, the Surveyor, began a separate new infirmary (now the University of Greenwich 'Dreadnought' Library). When it was completed in 1768 space freed in the main buildings allowed Pensioner numbers to exceed 2000.

Hospital food was plentiful if basic. Each man had 1 lb of meat a day (boiled or sometimes roast), beef three days a week and mutton on two, with pease-pottage on Wednesday and Friday. On those days there was also 8 oz cheese and 2 oz butter, and 4 oz cheese on others: 1 lb bread was served per man every day and half a gallon of beer. Tea joined the rations in the early nineteenth century, as it did in the Navy; also chocolate at breakfast, potatoes, and other improvements. Even then, cabbage was the only green vegetable, for two months in summer.

Left: No. 15 Cabin, Royal Charles Ward; a Pensioner's accommodation in the King Charles Court, from the *Illustrated London News,* 1865.
Right: The Anson Ward, with the figurehead of his round-the-world ship *Centurion;* only a fragment of this now survives. From the *Illustrated London News,* 1865.

The Painted Hall was built as the refectory with the officers eating in the railed-off Upper Hall. From 1708, Thornhill's work caused Pensioners' meals to be permanently moved to kitchen level in the undercroft below, and later also under the Chapel. Suitable inmates, paid £3 a year, helped in the service of beer and other kitchen duties; fair division of food was assured by one in each mess of four men taking it in turns to be served last.

From 1712 the Painted Hall was given up to the many visitors who soon flocked to see Thornhill's ceiling, paid the Hall keeper for the privilege and the printed description which the artist supplied, and thus launched Greenwich as a place of cultural tourism. They also launched what later became the Royal Hospital School; for it was from the Hall takings that the education of Greenwich Hospital boys was first supported, from about 1715. The Hall was subsequently only used for special occasions, the greatest being when the whole Hospital assembled on

4 November each year (William III's birthday, Old Style), to toast the royal founders.

STAFF AND DISCIPLINE

The Hospital had a huge staff and its own bakery and brewery, part of which survives and in 2010 reopened as a bar and restaurant for visitors to the site. The 'Military Department' was headed by the Governor, with Lieutenant-Governor, four Captains, eight Lieutenants and two chaplains. Under the Lieutenants senior Pensioners were appointed Boatswains, one to each ward with two mates to assist him. These had braided uniforms and ensured Pensioners shaved, looked after clothes and Hospital property and otherwise behaved. They also made sure all except the sick attended daily chapel on penalty of fine, or expulsion for the incorrigible. The Boatswains had 2s 6d (25p) and the Mates 1s 6d (7.5p) on top of the weekly shilling that all Pensioners received as 'tobacco money'; this only rose, to three, four and five shillings based on seniority, in 1860. On the 'Civil' side were the Secretary, Steward, Cashier, Clerk of the Cheque the Surveyor (architect) and Clerk of Works. There were also physician, surgeon, dispenser, six assistants and four matrons. All this fell under the Directors, who included the Governor and his deputy and the Treasurer. The last was sometimes a serving officer absent at sea, Admirals Sir Charles Saunders and Alexander Hood, Lord Bridport, being famous examples. In 1829 the Directors and the General Court were replaced by a board of five Commissioners responsible directly to the Admiralty.

'Battles by Sea and Land' 1801; a Greenwich and a Chelsea Pensioner swap yarns.

Discipline was naval (but no flogging) with fines, penalties, and loss of liberty to enforce good conduct among men who, if disabled, could be independent and rowdy . The patriarchal John Worley (1624–1721), one of the first Pensioners and Thornhill's model for 'Winter' in the Painted Hall, looked the part, but was drunken and coarse;

to be put in the confining house
for four days and each meal to be
exposed on an elevated place in

the hall...bread and water for a week and to wear the badge for swearing, to lose two [weeks'] allowance money and not to go out of the Hospital for one month...

He was then in his 80s, with seventy years at sea. Miscreants were first marked by wearing their coats inside-out but in the 1720s two dozen punishment coats of 'yellow stuff' were ordered. Wearers, dubbed 'canaries', had to do menial duties. By the 19th century the coats had red sleeves and were largely reserved for those found drunk on Sundays. Sir Thomas Hardy then earned further honour by abolishing them as unworthy of 'Greenwich heroes'. 'Boredom, listless idleness and mental vacuity' were Hospital life's real failings, noted the First Lord of Admiralty in 1864; 'it is not surprising that old sailors so circumstanced should resort to the ale-house, or to worse places.'

Top: A fifer and drummer of the Hospital band in the mid-19th century.
Below: Admiral Sir John Jennings, 1664–1743; the third and longest serving Governor, 1720–43; by Kneller.*

The first official recreation facility, from 1824, was a small library and reading room. In 1829 a monument, paid for by public subscription, was placed there to Charles Dibdin whose sea songs were said to have recruited more men for the Navy than the press gang. In about 1864 a skittle alley was installed in the 'chalk walk' (smoking area) under the Queen Mary colonnade. Bust and skittle alley are still there.

DEPENDANTS

While wives and families came in as visitors on many occasions including Founder's Day, they never lived in the Hospital (though widows employed as nurses were housed). As a result the Greenwich area became a community of families living apart from Pensioner husbands and many wives found domestic or similar work. Captain Marryat's Greenwich-based novel

'The Pensioner's Story'.
Visitors to the Hospital
engaged by the tale of an
ancient mariner. A late-19th
century painting by Thomas
Davidson.

Poor Jack (1840) gives a fictional case: Jack's father, having lost a
leg with Nelson at the Battle of the Nile gets a 'Hospital berth'
while his mother sets up a rented tea-room in Fisher's Alley, in the
shadow of the King Charles quarter. From 1730 Pensioners could
be 'chalked off' the dining roll in favour of a cash allowance, to eat
with and support families. Many, defeated by the type and
quantity of Hospital food, took advantage. Leftovers were also
distributed to the Greenwich poor.

'Out-pensions' of £7 a year, many recipients living locally,
were begun under an Act of 1763, made possible by growing
Hospital income and necessary by the Seven Years War. Extra
government funding was still needed and, though a modernizing
trend, out-pensioners became a financial burden. There were some
30,000 on the books by 1820, costing over £300,000 a year. In
1829 the costs were taken over entirely by Government.

This marked the passage towards the Hospital's closure. Before
1848 there was always a waiting list for entry but afterwards
vacancies increased rapidly. Four hundred beds were empty in

1853, 1100 in 1860. With the Navy enforcing the *pax Britannica* on the world's oceans, there were few candidates for Greenwich and being an out-pensioner was more attractive. In 1860 a Royal Commission proposed the end of in-pensions in exchange for an annuity to all existing inmates. In October 1865, under a new Act, 987 of the 1400 remaining in-Pensioners left the Hospital. In 1869 the last 'helpless' and incurables departed to other care, except a few remaining in the Infirmary. This was in turn taken over by the (merchant) Seamen's Hospital Society as the 'Dreadnought Hospital', replacing two hospital ships of that name, successively moored off Greenwich since 1827.

Wren's great complex then stood largely empty until the hitherto small Royal Naval College moved in from Portsmouth, in 1873. This steadily expanded at Greenwich, eventually becoming the 'Navy's university', while from 1982 the King Charles Court also housed the Joint Services Defence College. Finally, in 1998, nearly three hundred years of naval occupation came to an end when the two colleges moved out to new, purpose-built premises in Wiltshire. Leasehold management of the site then passed to the Greenwich Foundation for the Old Royal Naval College, a new management trust charged with the upkeep of the buildings under new uses, and the opening and interpretation of the site to the public. Wren's Hospital and College is now the Maritime Greenwich University Campus. Three of the main courts and the

Captain Cook, by Nathaniel Dance; painted in May 1776 between his leaving Greenwich and sailing on his last voyage.*

'Dreadnought' building are the headquarters campus of the University of Greenwich, which arrived in 2000. Trinity College of Music (now Trinity Laban), formerly in central London, has occupied the King Charles Court since 2001.

SHIPS THAT PASS

John Burnet's 1837 painting of 'Greenwich Hospital and Naval Heroes' (see cover), showing seamen marking the anniversary of Trafalgar in Greenwich Park, is a good example of the living history found in the Hospital. It includes named survivors from the Battle of the Nile and from the crew of *Victory* at Trafalgar; also

John Montagu, 1718–92, 4th Earl of Sandwich, by Thomas Gainsborough, with the Hospital shown behind.* *Right:* 'The Greenwich Pensioner'; a print of around 1800 illustrating Charles Dibdin's popular song of that title.

Nelson's servant Tom Allen, (who was admitted to Greenwich and buried there, although not a sailor) and Frank Cowell, last survivor of those ashore with Captain Cook at his death on Hawaii in 1779. When Queen Victoria visited the Hospital in 1840, it could still parade two hundred men who had fought all the great actions of the French Wars, 1793–1815.

Until 1743 the Hospital Governor was also Ranger of Greenwich Park and originally lived for some years in the Queen's House, whence the first, Captain William Gifford (1708–14) 'acquired' tapestries on his departure. Admiral Matthew Aylmer (Governor, 1714–20) began what became the Hospital School and welcomed the first Hanoverian king, George I, to England at Greenwich in September 1714. He also fitted up rooms in the King Charles Court as a 'VIP suite' and Greenwich became the regular station for the royal yachts until the end of sail, with frequent royal and diplomatic comings and goings. Admiral Sir John Jennings was the longest-serving Governor from 1720 to 1743 and saw the buildings nearly complete. In 1714 the Hospital bought an eleven-ton block of marble, seized by Admiral Rooke from a French prize and said to have been intended for a statue of Louis XIV: in 1735 Jennings personally paid Rysbrack £400 to carve it into the statue of George II in the Grand Square. If intended as royal flattery, it worked: that year brought the Hospital the Derwentwater estates.

Sir John Balchen's term as Governor was the shortest: April to June 1744. He was then sent back to sea for political reasons and drowned in October, when his flagship *Victory* was lost with all hands in the Channel. Sir William Hamilton, a son of his successor, became a notable diplomat whose wife, Emma, developed a passion for one Horatio Nelson. The regime of Admiral Isaac Townsend (1754–65) saw the disgraced Admiral Byng arrive under arrest in 1756. For over four months, Townsend held him in humiliating conditions in the Queen Anne attics, before he was court-martialled at Portsmouth for his failure to defend Minorca and shot, *'pour encourager les autres'* in the words of Voltaire, himself an earlier and admiring Greenwich visitor. A Pensioner who had been Byng's servant at the execution was still recounting his brave end, after 1800.

Admiral Rodney, famous in the War of American Independence, and Francis Holburne, were succeeded as Governors in 1771 by Sir Charles Hardy. His tenure saw the fire which wrecked the Chapel and in August

Captain Alexander Hood, 1727–1814, later 1st Viscount Bridport, by Sir Joshua Reynolds PRA. Hood was Hospital Treasurer and his widow presented the portrait to it.*

1775 James Cook, home from his second Pacific voyage, took up residence as a Hospital captain. 'It is a fine retreat', he wrote, 'and a pretty income, but whether I can bring myself to like ease and retirement time will show'. In July 1776 he made his final departure for the South Seas in the *Resolution* and *Discovery*. Nathaniel Portlock, who died in 1817 as a Hospital captain, sailed with him as a midshipman in *Discovery* and later commanded the *Assistant* on Bligh's second Pacific 'breadfruit' voyage, 1791–93.

Admiral Sir Hugh Palliser, who had been Cook's patron, was appointed Governor (1782–96) by his own backer, Lord Sandwich, First Lord of the Admiralty. Both were able but politically unpopular, from naval ructions of the American war. Palliser's gratitude left the Hospital one of its greatest paintings, Gainsborough's portrait of Sandwich, which he commissioned and presented. Princess Caroline of Brunswick landed in his time at Greenwich (1795) to marry the future George IV: 'What!' she was overheard to say (in French), 'Are all Englishmen missing an arm

Vice-Admiral Sir Thomas Hardy, 1769–1839. Nelson's friend, former captain of *Victory* and the Hospital's popular Governor from 1834; by Richard Evans.*

or a leg?'

Samuel, Viscount Hood, another great admiral of the American war was Governor from 1796, dying aged 92 in 1816. Nelson, a former protégé of his, stayed at Greenwich after loss of his arm in 1797 and lay in state in the Painted Hall following his own death at the Battle of Trafalgar. Thanks to adverse weather, his body arrived from the Nore after dark on Christmas night 1805 in the Admiralty yacht *Chatham*, manned by *Victory* men. It was discreetly borne up the foreshore and locked safely in the Hospital record room, off the Upper Hall, later dedicated to displaying Nelson relics. For three public days, 5–7 January 1806, over 30,000 people filed past the coffin in the black-draped Hall. It went up to the Admiralty at Whitehall in a great river procession on 8 January and after the burial in St Paul's Cathedral on the 9th the elaborate funeral carriage was brought back for display in the Hall until dismantled as 'decayed' in 1826. Two of Hood's successors, Sir Richard Keats (1821–34) and 'Nelson's Hardy', who followed him as Governor, were popular with the 'Sailor King' William IV, as was the Hospital. He had served under Keats, placed Chantrey's memorial bust of him in the Chapel and also

Nelson as a rear-admiral, after the Battle of the Nile in 1798, by L.F. Abbott. Based on a version done while he was staying with Lieutenant-Governor William Locker at the Hospital in 1797.*

paid at least three visits to Greenwich during Hardy's tenure, including on the 40th anniversary of the Battle of the Glorious First of June, 1794. On that occasion 176 Pensioners who had fought in it were among those who paraded, the king speaking to many of them with the habitual informality that exasperated his courtiers. Sir Robert Stopford (1841–47) further improved Pensioners' conditions and in 1844 presided over the award of Nelson medals (and 10 shillings each) to all those, about 350, who had fought with him, to mark the erection of Nelson's Column in Trafalgar Square the previous year. The last Governor, from 1853, was the one-legged Sir James Alexander Gordon. His Lieutenant-Governor was Sir William Edward Parry, the Arctic explorer. Just before the Hospital closed in 1869 Gordon died and was the last man to be interred in its old burial ground (by exception, since other burials there ended in 1857) alongside the present National Maritime Museum galleries and the 18th-century Mausoleum that holds Hood, Keats, Hardy and Portlock.

The Greenwich Hospital Collection

FOR 'EMINENT SERVICES'

The Hospital's role as a museum and art gallery sprang unforeseen from the decision to decorate the Painted Hall. Thornhill's long years of work, though not continuous, impeded its use as a Hospital dining room, for which it also became too small. Instead, in 1795, the newly arrived Lieutenant-Governor William Locker, Nelson's friend and former captain, suggested 'that it should be appropriated to the service of a National Gallery of Marine Paintings, to commemorate the eminent services of the Royal Navy of England'.

The French Wars had then already seen Howe's victory of 1 June 1794 and a 1795 bequest to the Hospital of pictures relating to the American war (of which Locker was a veteran) may have sparked the idea. In fact, its collection had begun in about 1711,

'The Battle of Trafalgar, 21 October 1805'. Painted by Turner for George IV in 1823–24, it proved so controversial that the King gave it to Greenwich Hospital six years later.*

when Thornhill had presented his oil study of
Pensioner John Worley and Mrs Clements gave it
John Greenhill's portrait of her husband, the first
Lieutenant-Governor. By 1795 other holdings
included further paintings, and more Thornhill
sketches for the Hall decoration presented in 1781
by James Stuart. Among other works, the Hospital
was given portraits of William and Mary by Kneller
in 1774, and Palliser's Gainsborough in 1783. His
later bequest included views of the siege of Quebec
(1759), a campaign in which both he and James
Cook had distinguished themselves. None the less,
Locker's idea lapsed until revived by his son.

E. H. Locker, about the time
of his retirement in 1844, by
H. W. Phillips.*

THE NAVAL GALLERY, 1824–1936

Edward Hawke Locker (1777–1849) is an important figure in the
Hospital's history. He was educated at Eton, went to sea as
secretary to Admiral Sir Edward Pellew (later Lord Exmouth), was
a Fellow of the Royal Society, a good amateur artist and a friend of
the writers Robert Southey and Walter Scott. He was also a skilled
administrator and well-connected.

'The Life of a Sailor' a self-
explanatory Victorian music
cover, about 1860.

In 1819 he became Secretary of
the Hospital and in 1829 its most
influential Commissioner. As
Secretary, he made three visits to its
Northern Estates resulting in
economic and social benefit to their
tenants in a depressed period. The
poisonous and by then unprofitable
lead-smelting plant at Langley was
closed, rents were lowered, roads
improved, and a lending library,
Friendly Society and savings bank
were formed with Hospital blessing at
Alston.

In 1823 he obtained agreement to
carry out his father's plan for the
Painted Hall, with the authoritative
backing of his friends Sir Thomas
Lawrence, President of the Royal
Academy, Francis Chantrey the
sculptor and Robert Smirke, architect

'The Naval Gallery' in the Painted Hall, 1865. L.H. Michael's drawing shows many identifiable pictures.*

of the British Museum. The tall lower windows were blocked up to give picture-hanging space and Locker began seeking gifts to fill it. (The only clearly identified official purchase was a portrait of Queen Anne from Greenwich parish church, for which the Admiralty approved payment of £10 in 1875.) Whether Locker spoke to George IV at Greenwich on his way to and from Scotland in 1822 is unknown, but the king backed and launched the scheme with a major gift of portraits from the Royal Collection, 38 items in all. Most arrived in 1824, including nearly all Lely's 'Flagmen' portraits of Restoration admirals, plus those which Kneller and Dahl had done for William III and Queen Anne. In 1829, the king added de Loutherbourg's great 'Battle of the First of June 1794' and its even greater pendant, Turner's highly controversial 'Battle of Trafalgar' completed in 1824. A five-year embarrassment in St James's Palace, it eminently suited Greenwich, though Pensioners continued to regale visitors (Turner included) with its nautical failings.

After this the Collection snowballed. Even before the railway reached Greenwich in 1836, it drew 50,000 visitors a year and eventually included 300 paintings. William IV gave seven pictures and some important ship models; Queen Adelaide donated his marble bust by Chantrey in 1841 and his portrait by Beechey in 1850. Locker begged Dance's portrait of Captain Cook (see p.17)

The Bombardment of Algiers, 1816, by George Chambers, painted for the Hospital in 1836. The attack liberated over 1000 Christian slaves.*

from the estate of Sir Joseph Banks in 1829 and in 1835 Mrs Cook's executor presented Zoffany's unfinished canvas of her husband's death on Hawaii. Locker himself gave eight pictures from 1823 to 1838, including his father's portrait by Gilbert Stuart and George Chambers' view of Admiral Vernon's capture of Puerto Bello in 1739, in which a Locker ancestor took the Spanish surrender, and which he commissioned. He was probably also behind this talented but short-lived painter's huge canvas of Lord Exmouth's 'Bombardment of Algiers, 1816', presented by those involved in 1836. This was one of several 'testimonials' painted for the Hall, including portraits of Sir Francis Beaufort, the hydrographer, and Sir James Ross, the Arctic explorer. Of six portraits by Reynolds, the finest are those of Alexander Hood, Lord Bridport (see p.19), given by his widow in 1825 and a 1779 canvas of the painter's friend Admiral Keppel, presented as late as 1939. Hood was Hospital Treasurer, one of many examples where personal links exist with Greenwich.

The most famous portrait of Nelson is Lemuel Abbott's of 1799, showing him after the Battle of the Nile (1798, see p.21), and the only one of many versions by Abbott showing him in a hat. This was presented by a number of subscribers in 1849 as one of an important group of paintings, of which the other six by Benjamin West and Richard Westall were painted to illustrate Nelson's 'official' biography in 1809.

In 1827 George Arnald's large picture of the French flagship *L'Orient* blowing up at the Nile was exhibited at the British Institution. This aristocratic body promoted history painting and Arnald's is one of four such 'patriotic' works which it commissioned for the Hospital (by competition) at 500 guineas each and presented to it between 1825 and 1835. In 1845 Prince Albert purchased (for £150) and presented the bullet-holed 'Trafalgar coat' in which Nelson was shot, after it was discovered in the family of one of Lady Hamilton's creditors. The breeches and stockings joined it in 1896, left by the daughter of the Royal Marine officer who had saved them from *Victory's* cockpit. The clothes, with portraits of all present, are shown in Arthur Devis's famous 'Death of Nelson' (1807) presented in 1825 by Nicholas Vansittart, Lord Bexley, who had been special envoy to the Danes in the events preceding Nelson's victory at the Battle of Copenhagen in 1801.

Apart from oil paintings, the Hall accumulated sculpture, drawings, ship models, and other items. This was quite separate from the large Royal Naval Museum, which arrived in 1873 with the Royal Naval College and displayed non-Hospital collections, including the Admiralty's extensive ship models, in seventeen rooms of the Queen Anne Court. In 1844, when Locker retired, the Hospital appointed an Honorary Curator with an annual gratuity of £100, to advise on what gifts to accept and to ensure care of its art collection. The first, still in post at his death in 1867, was the marine painter Clarkson Stanfield, who also oversaw repairs to the Hall itself and full panelling-out of the lower walls in 1845–46 to improve the display and accommodate the much increased number of pictures: previously they had only hung between the wall pilasters. After a gap until 1873 he was followed by similar artist-curators under the Naval College dispensation until 1904, and the Gallery remained

Below: **Nelson's Trafalgar coat, with the fatal bullet-hole in the left shoulder.***
Bottom: **The death of Nelson in *Victory's* cockpit by A. W. Devis, given to the Hospital in 1825 (detail). Captain Hardy stands on the right above (far right) Dr Beatty, with the Revd. Scott, left.***

open in the Painted Hall (with some items in the Naval Museum) until curatorial responsibility for the collection passed to the National Maritime Museum, as a permanent loan from Greenwich Hospital. This was officially founded in 1934 and opened at Greenwich in 1937. One or two pictures bought for the Museum in its formative period in the late 1920s also briefly hung in the Painted Hall before the Naval Gallery closed in 1936. Its contents then crossed the road to the Museum, with most of the Royal Naval Museum collection. The Painted Hall was restored to its present state and in 1939, after a break of over 230 years, it once more became a daily refectory for officers attending the Royal Naval College. While no longer in daily use for meals since the College left in 1998, it is still one of the most spectacular dining halls of Europe. With the Chapel, it is open daily to visitors and remains a venue for public and private dinners and other events. More recently the Nelson Room has also been reopened, with a display on the history of the Hall, including as the Naval Gallery.

'HMS *Devastation* at the Fleet Review for the Shah of Persia, 1873', by E. W. Cooke RA. *Devastation* was the Navy's first wholly steam-powered battleship. The picture was presented to the Naval Gallery by Thomas (later Lord) Brassey MP in 1875.*

Shield made from 125 unclaimed silver Naval General Service Medals of deceased Greenwich Pensioners for battles including those of 1 June 1794, St Vincent, Camperdown, the Nile, Trafalgar and Navarino. Made by order of the Admiralty, 1876.*

Cradle of the Navy

WESTON'S ACADEMY

The Hospital's 1694 charter had spoken of 'the maintenance and education of the Children of Seamen happening to be slain or disabled' in naval service. By August 1715 Governor Aylmer began diverting takings from the Painted Hall, Pensioners' fines and proceeds from the sale of stores, to educational ends. This supported the first ten sons of poor Pensioners at Thomas Weston's Academy in Greenwich, also feeding and clothing them. Uniform was modelled on the Pensioners' until 1756, when 'sailor's dress' with distinctive leather caps was adopted. Weston appears in his earlier Greenwich role of assistant to the first Astronomer Royal, John Flamsteed, in the Painted Hall ceiling. His good teaching included mathematics and fitted Greenwich boys for a sea career, from then on the general condition of a Hospital education. From 1720 about fifteen boys were boarded in the Hospital, under separate care from the Pensioners. By 1731, with wider naval entry than just Pensioners' sons, there were sixty and in 1748 a new ward was fitted for them in the Queen Mary Court.

THE FIRST SCHOOL

Ten years later, the first Hospital School building went up on the Pensioners' burying ground, north of Weston's Academy on modern King William Walk. Though solely for Hospital pupils it was run by Weston's successors until, in about 1779, the Hospital's insistence that its master, Thomas Furbor, devote himself solely to the 150 Hospital boys completed the split with the Academy. Probably the most significant Hospital School pupil of this period (in 1751–53) was Arthur Phillip, who in 1787–88 commanded the 'First Fleet' to Australia, founded modern Sydney and was first Governor of New South Wales until 1792. He died as an admiral in 1814.

The Hospital gave instruments to top boys of the School entering the Navy. This sextant was presented to Edmund Swain in 1844: he rose to Staff Commander by 1871 but died on active service shortly afterwards.

In 1782–84, William Newton, the Hospital Clerk of Works, put up an enlarged new School on the same site, with living accommodation for up to 200 boys. Over half this building still exists as a rear wing of what is now Devonport House (completed as a nurses' home in 1935). The School wing is now part of student accommodation for the University of Greenwich.

View of the NAVAL ASYLUM at Greenwich.

This is one of few images showing the Queen's House as the Naval Asylum and the only clear example that shows one of its 1807–09 wings before they were extended north (towards the background).

THE ASYLUM AND 'SCHOOLS'

In January 1821 the Hospital School was amalgamated, under the Greenwich Hospital Directors, with the adjacent and larger Royal Naval Asylum to become 'the Upper and Lower Schools of the Royal Hospital' – usually known as the Greenwich Hospital School (or Schools) until formally renamed the Royal Hospital School in 1892.

The Asylum started in Paddington in 1798 for the orphaned children of naval seamen, boys and girls, with entry fixed at between five and twelve years. It had powerful royal and naval backing (Nelson being a supporter) and a £40,000 endowment from Lloyd's. Early in 1806 George III granted it use of the Queen's House and its grounds at Greenwich, and 56 children moved in that December. Over fifteen years, Parliament supported expansion with £350,000 of aid. The colonnades and flanking wings were built from 1807, the House being earmarked for 300 girls and the wings for up to 700 boys. Total numbers were 800 by 1815. As originally completed in about 1809, the colonnades ended in short, balanced wings but these were lengthened northward by 1811: their upper floors were dormitories, with teaching, dining and other space below.

After 1821 the joint Schools fell under the superintendence of a captain of the Hospital, starting a division of naval management from teaching which only ended on retirement of the last Captain-Superintendent in 1945. Numbers rose to 1000, the Lower School being the 200 girls in the Queen's House and 600 Asylum boys: the Upper School was the 200 Hospital boys, who left Stuart's building, which became the School Infirmary. All boys were committed to enter sea service, specifically in the Navy after 1848 or, later and as an alternative, the Royal Marines. Edward Riddle, who wrote a standard work on navigation, was appointed to teach it as headmaster of what became the Upper Nautical School. He was there for thirty years (1821–51) and was succeeded by his son

John Riddle with his navigational pupils at the School in 1855.

John (–1856). The name 'Asylum' was formally dropped in 1825 and the sons of impoverished officers were allowed to join, though sons of warrant ranks were more common.

The more elementary and segregated girls' schooling ended in 1841 on grounds of 'evil communications'. The same year saw a mass protest of window-smashing by boys against a regime which, except for the brightest, was uninspired, tedious and forcefully disciplined. Reforms included innovations in industrial, nautical and physical training led by the new Lieutenant-Superintendent John Rouse and in 1851 an inspector reported that the Upper School was 'far beyond any other known to me in scientific attainment'. Much of this was due to the teaching improvements brought about by the Revd George Fisher, a well-known astronomer, overall Headmaster and Chaplain from 1834, and Principal, 1860–63. In the 1880s better physical care and more nautically directed 'trades' training made pupils an asset to all branches of the Navy. Over 10,000 boys from Greenwich joined from 1874 to 1930; of these, five became admirals. In 1886 the School also absorbed that of Sir William Boreman's Foundation, established in Greenwich in 1672 for the sons of local seamen, fishermen and watermen. 'Boreman boys', up to a hundred at a time, became part of the Upper School. They wore distinctive badges and unlike the others were day pupils and not obliged to join the Navy , though many did. The last, George Berry, left to join as an apprentice engineer in 1931 and was lost with HMS *Prince of Wales* in 1941.

School life at Greenwich was none the less spartan,

regimented, and conducted 'at the double'. It was largely cloistered inside the grounds and self-sufficient: the boys did the cleaning, laundry, baking, tailoring and so on as 'trades' training, though this modified over time. For many it was still an improvement on the hardship from which it relieved them. About seventy old boys of the 1920s, who joined the School at Greenwich by the age of eleven and left at fourteen of fifteen, were still alive when this account first appeared in 1994: many then still testified to what the School gave them and to its *esprit de corps*.

Revd George Fisher (1794–1873); a photograph taken about 1860.

GREENWICH AND HOLBROOK

From 1862 to 1876 the buildings reached the full extent of what is now the National Maritime Museum. The first of three drill or 'block' ships was built in front of the Queen's House in 1842. The last, called *Fame* (1873), with many other ancillary buildings, was demolished when the School left for its new home in Suffolk in 1933, where its figurehead still looks out over the playing fields.

In 1919 Gifford Sherman Reade (1845–1929) a wealthy ship owner and planter living in New Zealand, gave his 850-acre Holbrook estate near Ipswich to the Admiralty, in gratitude for the preservation of his ships in the First World War. His wish, in agreeing its transfer to Greenwich Hospital for School use, was to contribute to the future strength of the Navy. He also bequeathed half his fortune, though not until the capital had accumulated for eleven years after his death. After a design competition, buildings were commissioned from a firm of Birmingham architects in 1924, but it was only Reade's 1928 decision to leave the Hospital his entire fortune of over £1m that tipped the balance to proceed on the planned scale.

On 26 October 1928, the Duke of York, later King George VI, laid the foundation stone of the Royal Hospital School, Holbrook, a striking Queen Anne-style complex overlooking the River Stour, with a 200-foot central clock-tower, accommodation for 850 boys, and echoes of Greenwich both in its buildings and layout. One of its many advantages (apart from country air) was that boys now lived in eleven houses rather than the mass barrack conditions of Greenwich. The

The School entrance, about 1906, with the drill-ship *Fame* and the Queen's House behind; from a Greenwich postcard.

31

Greenwich Hospital schoolboys, photographed in the 1850s.

buildings in Greenwich which the School had vacated were taken over by the National Maritime Museum.

The School opened in 1933 and remained a largely technical one until after the Second World War, when the condition that boys enter the Navy was suspended and the military superintendence gave way to civilian teaching management. The education was still elementary and 'secondary-modern', and policy deliberately shifted at this time to build up a more academic, 'grammar-school' stream. Though slow and costly this was considered vital to benefit boys of all abilities. The School gained its first A-level success and university place in 1953, and many since.

In subsequent years, however, the decline of seafaring as a national occupation steadily reduced the pool from which the School could draw pupils. In 1990 a new Act of Parliament allowed it to accept both boys and girls from other backgrounds, though favouring those of seafaring families. The School is now an HMC, independent, coeducational boarding and day school, with a proud naval heritage and a modern outlook. It has a capacity of some 770 boarding and day pupils, and in 2010 will have completed an £18-million renovation of its boarding houses, and the building of a new music school. All pupils now pay fees but the Hospital continues to subsidize a significant number of seafaring children through bursaries. In future years the School is expected to become increasingly financially independent from Greenwich Hospital.

THE INVISIBLE HOSPITAL

Since the Pensioners left Greenwich in 1865–69, the Hospital has developed as a substantial charitable organization, with an updated welfare and educational role. This has been possible through its fortunate inheritance of a range of assets, all under professional management. The Hospital's status is that of Crown charity, of which the Secretary of State for Defence is the sole Trustee on behalf of the Crown. The constitution of Greenwich Hospital is set out in the Royal Charter of 1694 and in the Greenwich Hospital Acts 1865 to 1996. When the Hospital was founded its trustees were the Greenwich Hospital Commissioners. Following the Greenwich Hospital Act 1865 this responsibility was transferred to the Admiralty and then in 1964 to the Secretary of State for Defence, following the re-organization of what is now the Ministry of Defence (MoD).

The Royal Hospital School at Holbrook, Suffolk, with Alton Water behind. The playing fields on the left run down to the Stour estuary.
Courtesy: Royal Hospital School.

Oversight of Hospital affairs is through the Admiralty Board of the Ministry of Defence, their direct management being by a small staff under the Director of Greenwich Hospital, a post established in 1884.

Greenwich Hospital receives no public funding. Its financial capital, built up since the 18th century, today comprises quoted investments and property. The Northern Estates, where land has been both bought and sold since the 18th century, comprise farms, mineral resources (excluding coal) and sporting rights. Once much more extensive, these have shrunk to less than 6000 acres in Northumberland and the Borders and now form only a modest part of the overall assets.

The Hospital also derives income from the rents of commercial and residential property in Greenwich, including Greenwich Market, and from other properties in London and elsewhere. It has no income from the National Maritime Museum or the Old Royal Naval College (ORNC), although it remains the freeholder of the latter, which is on a 150-year lease to the Greenwich Foundation for the ORNC. The Hospital's accounts are audited by the National Audit Office and laid annually before Parliament.

THE MODERN CHARITABLE ROLE

Over 300 years from its foundation, Greenwich Hospital continues to perform its charitable role in accordance with the principles set out in the Royal Charter of 1694.

It still helps serving and retired Royal Navy and Royal Marines personnel and their dependants, caring for the elderly, supporting the widowed and educating the young. The wide scope of its

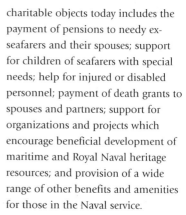

charitable objects today includes the payment of pensions to needy ex-seafarers and their spouses; support for children of seafarers with special needs; help for injured or disabled personnel; payment of death grants to spouses and partners; support for organizations and projects which encourage beneficial development of maritime and Royal Naval heritage resources; and provision of a wide range of other benefits and amenities for those in the Naval service.

The Hospital has also been instrumental in the creation, for the Admiralty Board, of the new Royal Navy and Royal Marines Charity, which from 2010 has become the Navy's prime charity for the 21st century, and the major conduit for Greenwich Hospital's charitable output to seafarers.

Separately, in addition to running the Royal Hospital School, the Hospital also maintains sheltered housing for eligible former Royal Naval and Royal Marines personnel. Its first purpose-built housing scheme, Greenwich Court, opened in Southsea in 1989. The second, Greenwich Place, was opened in Saltash, Cornwall, in 1994 – the Hospital's 300th anniversary year. HRH The Duke of York, then a serving naval officer, performed the ceremony and also became the Hospital's first formal Royal Patron that year. On the Navy's departure from Greenwich in 1998, the Hospital reclaimed a fine early 19th-century building there, the Trafalgar Quarters – originally Hospital offices – and converted it into a third residence. This opened in 2001, bringing 'Greenwich pensioners' back to the site for the first time since 1869. All three residences comprise a range of double and single apartments, providing high-quality, manager-assisted accommodation and excellent support facilities.

In these ways the royal connection remains and Greenwich Hospital continues to serve seafarers and their dependants, as it has for over three centuries. In 2012 Greenwich itself becomes a Royal Borough, exactly 300 years since Thornhill's scaffolding was removed from the Painted Hall of the Hospital, to reveal its royal founders, William and Mary, enthroned in its ceiling. If their shades still look down, both would surely approve.

Top: **George Huff, resident of Trafalgar Quarters since 2001. His WWII service on destroyers, corvettes and submarines took him to Singapore, America, Canada, Africa and the Red Sea. As a RN Reservist, he was also called up in 1962 during the Cuban missile crisis. On leaving the Navy he was a contract electrician for Watney's brewery.**
Courtesy: Greenwich Hospital.
Above: **Pupils of the Royal Hospital School enjoy splendid sailing facilities.**
Courtesy: Royal Hospital School.